THEM

ISSUE ONE
Fall 2013

FOUNDING EDITOR

Jos Charles

EDITOR

Jamila Cornick

EDITOR

Emerson Whitney

Cover design, issue layout, and introduction by **Jos Charles**.

Text set in Goudy Old Style, Times, and IM Fell Great Primer.

WEB: themlit.com
EMAIL: themliterature@gmail.com
FACEBOOK: facebook.com/themlit
TWITTER: twitter.com/themlit

All Copyrights are retained by the original authors and artists. THEM retains Archival and Anthology rights.

ISBN: 978 – 1 – 304 – 71298 – 1
ISSN: 2332 – 0354

©2013

ON TRANS*

"Trans*" is an umbrella term meant to include not just transgender identities, but any person who does not exclusively identify as the gender assigned at their birth. This often includes genderqueer, bigender, agender, genderfuck, and other gender-variant identities. Like with any umbrella term, the only way to know if "trans*" applies to someone is if they apply it to themselves.

THEM uses the word "trans*" in an attempt to make room in the old, reconcile, carve, and begin from where we can. That is to say "trans*" is not perfect and without limits; THEM adopts it as a strategy—contingently and consciously. If a more suitable term, less grounded in binarist western identity-politics emerges, THEM will be happy to abandon "trans*" and utilize another.

THEM is not the gender police. Authors and artists herein may not identify with "trans*" as a term, i.e. folks with cultural gender identities who reject its use. Likewise not all writing herein may be considered "trans* writing." THEM is willingly confused by what does or doesn't pass as trans* writing. THEM is critically ambivalent. THEM is happy to present conflicting manifestos.

ON SUBMISSIONS
a note from the Founding Editor

It was my hope with THEM to facilitate a space that prioritizes writers who address trans* bodies in their complexities—work that doesn't appeal to "being trans*" as if it were one neat, complete narrative. No one is "just trans*". Race, class, ability, and sexuality are just some of the intersections that constitute the violence trans* folks face. To address trans* bodies as they are engendered without accounting for how they are racialized, sexualized, colonized, and/or colonizing is to default to normative and oppressive ways of identifying bodies.

To that end this collection could be labeled "experimental", but only insofar as trans* bodies are consistently maligned as "experimental". If the work herein tends to move outside of convention, it is less due to a pretense of "challenging our audience" than of challenging normative meanings mobilized against other ways of making sense. What follows is less an "experiment" in form as a documentation of bodies, interrogating the differing ways we come to understand, desire, and survive.

THEM thanks its readers and every body that scavenges.

In love & solidarity,

Jos Charles

CONTENTS

Boston Davis Bostian
- 11 bLACK boxes
- 12 define: TraNsition
- 14 body

Brody Wood
- 15 LEVELING UP

Calvin Gimpelevich
- 18 INNOVATION, REVERSAL, AND CHANGE

Cassady Bee
- 25 NO ONE WATCHES TELEVISION ANYMORE

Codi Suzanne Oliver & Willow Heatley
- 26 APRIL

Gi Keer
- 37 *from* NOTHING IS MISSING

Grey Vild
- 42 IF SHE ALWAYS
- 45 A DISGUST
- 47 SOUND THE OCEAN
- 48 STATICS
- 50 AN ELEGANT REFUSAL
- 52 WITH THE NERVES LIT

H. Melt	54	I AM NOT TALKING ABOUT GAY MARRIAGE
Janani Balasubramanian	56	MAYBE A LITTLE GIRL WILL KILL ME TOMORROW
j/j hastain	62	ALLEYWAY
	64	GETTING TO KNOW YOU
	66	"UNDER THE FULL MOONLIGHT WE DANCE"
Joy Ladin	68	LETTER TO THE RADFEMS
Levi Sable	71	GLITTER ON THE DANCE FLOOR
Lucas Scheelk	87	THINGS I WISH I COULD ENJOY AGAIN [...]
Mx Glass	88	AMERICAN CROW
	89	ERRARE
reba overkill	90	ARCHITECTURE
	91	ROUND, HOPEFUL POEM
	92	MY POWERS ARE AWAKENING

Rex Leonowicz	93	ART AND SEX ALONG THE NEW YORK WATERFRONT
	95	where are your feelings? [...]
Stephen Ira	97	This Year When [...]
Van Binfa	98	FOUR YEARS

bLACK boxes

this is a love letter. a request for you-me to let me down lightly like /likely/ a black coffin with green sateen sheet. a rebirth into me. this seedy night. like a pen-point. pinpoint: a lighthouse on the beach. light a candle. a silver needle. silver wheeling. reeling brain. each man a spoke in my wheeling brain. stand tall marine. take one for the team. dwindled down. whittled down candle. alight with air. a silver needed. silver wheel. self is to Heather as Boston is to night. or light, i can't decide which. the highpitched ice did birth me as Boston. lost in this seedy night. loft in a fright. my studio freight train. where I retrain my fears. due to a pair, down. pare down the Corps. it's not for women worn. just lay down, let your weary self be taken. raped in the militant night. the seeds inside you birth you to needle light. like a wheel. silver so let my self emerge ::between ashes and north rock. this is for [get]-ing my self, as in: to receive. this is for [get]-ing myself, as if: from lack. or perhaps this is just a way to forget my self. like spellbound, a nation believing we liked it, we asked for it, we wanted it more. so send us on leave: homeward bound. you've done your duty, marine. stand down. for many years I've watched the

                        black

                                  boxes

                                          down

define: TraNsition

TraNs: with the sense   'beyond,   outside-of,
through, over,
              from
              one state/to another,
                                    on-the-far-side-of'

with the sense   'sur>passing, TraNscending,

as TraNshuman': beyond the human,
                                    superhuman.

TraNshistorical: that TraNscends the
                                    universal
                                    or
                                    [eternal.

TraNsitory: it won't *last*.

                        TraNsitive: to be able to   pass.

a red blooming. TraNs<illum>inate: to cause   light

to pass through.   to go beyond   (an: orange moon).

            to go across. perhaps,   ...at all costs.

TraNsient: passing by or |a|w|a|y| momentary,   fleeting.

    TraNsillience: a leaping.

        TraNsillient: to leap across, skip over, <omit>.

           [then] TraNsit: the carr/y/ing...   to place.

TraNsindividual: not confinded.
                a-blue-un-binding.   t o   taste

TraNscendency. to face TraNsiency: this brief ["i"]
                an awaken>ing, embraced.

in truth: a body left behind. [or.]

            TraNsition: a state of grayce.

                                                                            body

<withering> a-long.   whe/ther the grass_shines

in the _{metal}   light-like green   [alum]inum, or not.

weather)ed,   the plastic chair

                                        you-did it in. I'm gone.

Perhaps, a   song: Dear father,

          will you   need   the gun after your last job?

We fought> *"our way."*

                                    The displ[lay]

on mom's lawn is *red_and_hot*.   But-that morn/ing,
you read

<a passage from the Bible, and a> small ^{devotion}_{al}, it said:

Today,
is a good day. And
                then
                    you
                    brought
                            the
                                pistol
                                    to your head.

LEVELING UP
Brody Wood

You say you're gonna take me to your parents' restaurant, that I'll drink on the patio and that it will feel good. I have wanted that. At your 16th birthday party, your mom offered me her bathing suit so I could swim in the pool. I might put money on her having a succulent reaction to what has become of me, as the person she may remember as your young friend. Am I a betting man, though? Do I need to know how well my teenage breath permeates through and levels up to how I honestly swill the idea of you around in my mouth, now? Do I need to name the ways we both grew up? I hull away my body and I put it back a lot and I choose resilience and elasticity. Automatically. No question.

When we were kids, you were in love with my best friend, and I was in love with your best friend. Now I want to be your man.

Before today, I wanted to tell you that I needed space from you, so that I could be with this until it went away, so that you didn't look at it when it was ostensibly thriving, but I didn't need to tell you that I needed space because you gave me that, because you didn't call. I thought I would give this up. I thought I would want to stop. I knew that I wouldn't want you to look at me any differently. Then you called, and now I want to be your man. With bells on, me on my ass. You saw we kept missing each other, truncated that absence, and made a time and a place, and we spent a couple hours there and we made a room for ourselves there, and I give the name *corset* to my systematic and earnest need to see two men be gentle with each other, if we treat each other right, and the corset is ongoing in that room. Now I consider regressing the hard lines I started making. I consider not giving this up. Not wanting to stop. Being your man. I won't want you to look at me any differently.

Would I give you a break if you did? Do I give you a break any other way? Do I give you a break for being a different kind of man than me? What would it mean if I did? What would become of being rivals with you? What will become, if your pleasure levels up to mine, of the possibility that we are ill-fitting to each other?

I give the name *undoing* to the walls I rinse with the love I forage, and to the reciprocity that comes in smooth strides in the face of being old friends. I trap the accomplishments and undo years, but it takes the most time to undo this summer.

I wanted to be able to choose whether or not to reconcile this without you and without disclosure. I got that, and I think I am choosing to say this to you, that the countenance of my love is full of something more, bigger than gossip but smaller than threat, that I consider actually being your man. I choose to disclose the legwork of this love, the work of my love, I work at love, I have worked at love, as an adult, and it drives a piece of composure into me, a line that is trying to be hard, that I don't need anything from you.

INNOVATION, REVERSAL, AND CHANGE
Calvin Gimpelevich

You wake up one morning to find your body larger and hairier than previously recalled. Your hands seem twice—more, three times!—their normal size and your knees creak when moved. Your stomach is thick with muscles and fat.

You swing your legs over the side of the bed and push yourself up. Your lower back hurts and your vision has blurred. Faded tattoos mark your arms beneath the coarse hair matting everything but your palms. There are no mirrors in the room, so you touch your face with meaty new hands. Your fingers are calloused and you don't know your strength, so you end up hurting your face. On touching the top of your head you realize you are bald.

You went to bed as a six-year-old girl.

The loss of your hair is, perhaps, the greatest tragedy because you had only just grown your bangs out enough that they could be tied into a ponytail. To have your bangs snatched from you so soon after this victory (which took months of waiting) is tragic, the greatest loss since Marc Anthony the hamster died.

You are curious about your situation, but not overly concerned. Your mother had warned you that before you turned into a grown-up your body would go through a series of strange and unappealing changes. She did not elaborate, but it stands to reason that becoming a middle-aged man is yet another step in the winding path to womanhood.

Your biggest concern is that you have a dance recital in under a week, and you don't think that Madame Danvers will understand your being a middle-aged man. This is because you overheard your mother telling your best friend Cindy's mother that Madame Danvers only teaches dance because she is barrel and can't abuse children of her own. The critique is apt, she looks like a barrel, not at all like the soft curves that every woman and Disney princess should have. You reason the problem came with this stage, either Madame Danvers missed it or became stuck. Adults are often unsympathetic to the plight of stages they did not have. Like how your mother can't understand the tragedy of an incomplete princess doll set when she had had none.

You decide to find your mother and ask her advice about the new stage. A pink butterfly clock hangs from your wall. It is seven-thirty and you are good at reading the clock. Your mother should be just rising from bed.

You exit your room and attempt to walk down the stairs. You aren't successful. Your legs and feet are large and ungainly; you bump into the railing and trip over your feet. You stumble into the banister's curve and fall down, limbs sprawled beyond grace. At least the extra fat has padded your fall.

Your finger hurts. There is blood. You run into your parents' room shouting "Mommmmy" in baritone. Your mother shouts with surprise, and pulls her lace robe shut. She screams for your father and rushes into the bathroom, slamming the door.

Your father rushes up shouting. You try to explain what is going on, but he just keeps yelling. Tears of frustration well up in your eyes and thick, wet sobs soon rack your body. Unable to stand the chaos of your house you rush from your home, wearing only the ripped and stretched unicorn pajamas worn to bed.

People give you strange looks in the world, they stand back and stare. Tears continue to fall from your eyes, but you begin to regain your composure. You often cry when frustrated, but never for long. Sometimes you stretch the tears for a sympathy cupcake, but there are no parents to bribe you with candy now. This recharges the tears.

You walk and walk, unsure of where you are going. Before long you are lost. Your try retracing your steps, because that's what your teacher always says to do when you're lost. Either stay put and wait for your parents or retrace your steps if your parents won't know where to find you.

You are tired and hungry—you didn't get to have breakfast despite its being the most important meal of the day—and very lost. Hot tears flow. Luckily, your new body is much hardier than your old one. In your normal body, you probably would have collapsed from exhaustion by now.

The new area you've stumbled into is much dirtier than where you live. Broken bottles litter the street and shabby people just sit there on the sidewalk. They look like the people your mother warns you never to get close to because they're icky and do strange things. Sometimes your father drops a few coins in front of them, but mostly he just ignores them. These areas have always frightened you before.

Your emergency training has reached a contradictory place. You're supposed to ask a grown-up for directions, but you're also supposed to stay away from strangers. You think very hard, trying to decide which rule to break. The decision is made for you when a friendly lady walks up to you and says hello.

"Hello," the word comes out strange. "Can you help me?"

"Of course I can, honey." The woman is wearing lipstick the same shade as you got for Christmas last year. And she put about as much on as you did before your mom wiped a bunch of it off. "Follow me and we can talk."

Relieved, you follow her into one of the buildings. It's about as dirty inside as it is outside, and the lady seems to know everyone there. You're trying very hard to remember your mother's cell number. She made you memorize it in case of an emergency, and this is definitely an emergency.

You and the lady enter a small room with very little furniture. An old bed takes up most of the space, but at least it seems cleaner than the rest of the building. You start asking about a telephone, but the lady has placed her hand between your legs and all of a sudden something is happening down there that has never ever happened before. A strange tingling sensation becomes present where her hand is and something, something strange that wasn't there before, yet is attached to you, begins to move and feel odd.

Baffled and frightened, you bolt. The lady calls after you, but you've already run out of the building and into the street.

You want to cry, you should be crying, but something has changed in your body. No matter how hard you try, the tears do not come. Instead you feel rage. The sensation builds, starting in your core and builds out. You know anger, frustration, and rage. You know to scream and kick your limbs out.

One of the shabby men approaches you and your tantrum. You are so frustrated you push with all of your might and instead of laughing or looking chagrined he lifts into the air and flies back, literally flying for a few static seconds, before crashing into the ground. This is your power.

Frustration ebbs from the shock of what you've just done. All your life you've exerted your will on the world, but never had such success. You are frightened and confused, but these are dwarfed by the sated anger. You almost feel good. There is a connection to this new body. You are a six year old girl in the shell of a physically impressive man. The distinctions between your mind and your body are blurred. You are young and old and strong and weak.

You are, in short, a conundrum.

NO ONE WATCHES TELEVISION ANYMORE

Cassady Bee

This space is silent.

Dramatic and casual

Like Surgery On TV,

On mute.

Did you know

Your brain can't process light?

It just absorbs the stimuli,

And is transfixing—

Like blankly watching fire.

APRIL
Codi Suzanne Oliver & Willow Healey

Establish a conduit

Two weeks ago while I was bike riding around in the sun, I traveled under a bridge and found a girl I kind of knew. We exchanged names, Arin and Willow. We talked about drugs, modeling, and kink for 2 hours. We went and shared a pizza because we were enjoying each other's company. She invited me out to a 'kegger' and we planned to meet up after I went and napped. I went home and fell asleep hoping she wouldn't feel bad that I wasn't coming. I woke an hour later. There was a can of beer in the snack cabinet so I put it in the freezer with the intent to drink it. It had been there since before I left for Toronto 9 months ago, having since returned. I asked nobody in particular if it had a specific purpose, or if it's just been forgotten for so long. In any case, I resolve, my father will either think my brother drank it or he won't care. I think my father realizes I've been stealing beers and liquor for a long indeterminate amount of time and he probably doesn't care.

I don't have a brand of cigarettes that I strongly prefer over others. The last time I bought cigarettes I asked the clerk for whatever is cheap and he sold me a pack of Newports for $11 when I could see Marlboros advertised for $9.

The washing machine makes noises like a whimpering dog, I keep looking up thinking my dog is whimpering. My dog makes me sad because she seems bored and lonely all the time. I don't make an effort to spend time with her that much.

It's funny to internalize the idea that gender is a social construct and then talk about a dog or any animal.

Last Friday, I had stolen a watermelon from a fancy grocery store after a doctor's appointment. I carried the watermelon around all day with the intention of finding someone to eat it with me. I wanted to videotape myself throwing it against a wall and then ravenously eating the chunks. I didn't end up finding anyone to eat it with me. I sat by the river. I played music on my headphones. I wanted to go sit inside and share my watermelon so I went to a coffee shop that I like. I like it because everyone who works there smiles at me.

Somewhere else, Willow and I are sitting silently in a 24 hour diner at 5am, really 'fucked up' looking (dirt, muddy shoes, unkempt hair, smeared makeup) staring into our cups of coffee, both with plates of uneaten breakfast food in front of us. Willow leans over and spits on the floor, nobody notices. I say "ow" as I lift my cup to drink from it. My friend Arin shows up by coincidence. We drink coffee and eat the watermelon with a hunting knife. We talk about drugs and our weeks. She tells me about her working as a porn star with a "really amazing" company. I vocalize my interest. Arin phones up her boss right then and tells him to give me an interview. He agrees. Arin's friend texts her asking if she knows where to find MDMA. She phones up her dealer and asks him to deliver some MDMA. Arin's friend, Michael, shows up and catches my eye. I am pleasantly surprised when he sits down beside us. I tell him that he is "a beautiful creature" and Arin agrees. We go outside so they can smoke cigarettes and I can wait for the bus. The dealer arrives and Arin disappears for 5 minutes or so. Michael and I talk about a local gay bar and decent places to go dancing. Arin returns and gives Michael his MDMA. Arin and I plan to meet the following afternoon so she can take me to my interview. My bus arrives in the distance. I give Arin a hug goodbye. Michael quietly asks me for a hug and then brushes it off when I don't respond. I get on the bus. I think that was in Milwaukee, Wisconsin. I was by myself.

I saw a bear/'daddy' type man on the bus. Was aware that he would be considered attractive by several of my friends. The people I have sex with tend to be completely unlike the 'daddy' type. A secret to success in political queer spaces is that you may talk a great deal about your sexual identity, but it is best not to mention your sexuality.

I get up the next morning. I pay close attention to putting on my makeup so it looks decent for my interview. I am uncertain what to wear to an interview for becoming a porn star. I decide to just wear what I would usually wear. You're not allowed to think about fucking me.

Now, if instead of living here in a dorm room with a person I've never talked to before and have no intentions of talking to again, I lived in, possibly, a "punk house" (put in scare quotes due to my own ambiguous and multiple interpretations of aesthetic subcultures) with four or five other people, then instead of typing this I might be organizing a show or planning a trip to a food drop-in with a housemate of mine. In any case, a show is being planned for our basement and one of the housemates, a cisgender woman named Dalia, informs me that one of the booked bands frequently performs a song entitled "Punk is For Clits" which she, the housemate, worries is a well-intentioned yet cissexist response to misogyny in the punk scene in whatever city we might be living in, let's say Detroit. Another housemate announces that her ex-partner Matt is not to be allowed into the house at any point, even for the show, and that he must be told so by one of the other housemates. The task is left to Saul as ze is the closest with Matt and an ex-housemate of his. Matt, in response to this news, bans Saul and all of the occupants of this house from his own house, which upsets myself and Saul the most. At the show Dalia asks the booked band not to play the aforementioned song, citing the reasons why it is cissexist. The singer of the band (who is presumably the lyricist) responds saying that she cannot be cissexist because she is bisexual. They play the show and respect Dalia's request, but we later find bathroom graffiti referring to everyone in the house as a "PC Cunt". Three days later, the band announces that they have broken up. Dalia and I are stigmatized by the majority of straight punks in Detroit and we can find little reason to leave the house, avoiding shows and unable to go to Matt's house, where most of our friends live. We have no money to pay for access to spaces like bars or clubs or restaurants. We entertain ourselves by starting a housemate noise band and watching Neon Genesis Evangelion. We feed ourselves mostly on the food drop-ins that Saul and I attend and from dumpster diving vegan/organic health food stores. We are all the same size and we collectivize our clothing. In seven months we watch seventeen series of anime and we haven't spoken to any person outside of our house except for a few international friends we have made on the internet, collectively using one Facebook account and one Twitter feed to interact with them. They are aware that we are 5 or 6 people but they never ask which of us they are talking to. The internet continues to work even though the electricity has been shut down. Our landlord forgets we're there. Clothing seems to find its way into our house, or to materialize from nothing. We leave only to do things that I can't write about because cops read all our blog posts. We forget our own and each other's names, interests, histories, genders, and aesthetics. Our politics are all one in the same. Living human bodies find their way into our house or materialize from nothing. We look like where the sky meets the lake at night. Quinn told me about a dream that they had that I won't write about because they might use it in something later. But we talked about how we and many people in our circle fantasize about transcendence. I think I know what they mean by "in our circle," like, antagonistic/"nihilistic" (scare quotes because it has many connotations and variations and I'm not sure which I'm utilizing here) gender nonconforming people whose primary endeavor is to destroy (or maybe not destroy, maybe just leave) corporeality and language and etc.

Mark and I are walking along the lakefront smoking cigarettes. It is one of the first warm nights of the spring and many people are outside, some with fires, some with food. The sun has gone down by now and we are walking north, past the scattered groups of picnickers so Mark can smoke weed. We had bought snacks at a convenience store. We find a quiet spot and sit down on the stone steps that line this part of the lake. Mark uses the light of his cell phone to see as he packs a bowl. I let Mark borrow my lighter and help block the wind while he smokes. I sit down and eat my hot cheetos and drink my iced tea and we talk about something. A group of three teenagers sit down about 30 feet from us. Mark mentions seeing one of them try to light a joint. Mark smokes more. One of the teenagers approaches us and asks to borrow our lighter. I hand him my lighter. Mark and I follow him to his friends and Mark shares his weed with them. They mention something about it being the season when travellers begin to appear in Wicker Park and I talk about my friends who are trainhopping to British Columbia. We finish talking and Mark finishes smoking with them and we continue to walk north. We smoke cigarettes and talk about gay club culture. A group of four people in sleeping bags and blankets ask to bum cigarettes. Mark and I each give them two cigarettes. They talk about the Night Ministry bus [a bus that provides food and clothing to homeless people] in Boystown [Chicago's gay bar district]. We tell them about the Take Back Boystown initiative and the Northalsted Business Alliance and racism in the neighborhood. One of them mentions being harassed for kissing her boyfriend and her girlfriend in public. She talks about getting harassed for being in the Night Ministry line. She says "The thing about trannies is that they're all jealous of real women" and Mark fakes a phone call and we quickly walk away. We talk about what she had said and the complicated power dynamics of the conversation. We walk to a park where Mark had once gone while on acid and Mark tells me about the experience.

Role

While I wait for Arin to show up, a man asks me if I go to the college that is on my linen tote bag. I tell him that I do not and that the bag is from a girl that I use to date. This is partly untrue.

He looks at me awkwardly and briefly wide-eyed. He says "Well, whatever your into" and looks uncomfortable. We stand in silence at a distance that indicates my distaste and serves only to make him more uncomfortable. I see Arin in the distance and wave at her. We start talking and she tells me about how she did MDMA, Cocaine, and Ketamine with Michael and his girlfriend the previous evening. She found the Ketamine on the floor of the club they were dancing at. We go to eat food and talk animatedly about the differences and similarities between pharmaceutical and street drugs. We take the train to the train station that is closest to the studio. I tell Arin that I am excited and pleasantly curious about the interview.

We arrive at the doors to the studio. I am surprised at how understated the outside of the studio looks. The day is hot, dry, and slightly sticky with sweat. Arin and I walk inside the doors and into the dimly lit room.

Penny Goring said 'and codi, "they" try to make us fear the future .. i've got nothing and i've also got minus nothing, and it is OKAY. there is no such thing as the future. well, i haven't found it yet.'. Hel said 'people aren't things, people are people' but she was aware that she arrived to this conclusion anecdotally and that it doesn't really mean anything and that it's an impossible idea to actualize until after [something/"the revolution"/liberation/the end of capitalism/the end of cissexism]. I don't remember how I felt about it at the time but since then I've started going by "it" pronouns even though nobody calls me that. Willow said 'Be intentional with your intensity.'

The five of us lie side-by-side next to each other in a twin-sized bed and there isn't enough room for comfort, and we're each sobering at our own slow pace, pretending to sleep, thinking about how in 'the morning' (or whatever might resemble the morning), whenever we get out of this bed, we will have to account for the night and the sex and assess the role the drugs had to play in it and how we feel about it and continue our relationships to one another from this point of information (as each moment or series of moments or event is a point that informs our relationships to one another, seems obvious but worth mentioning) and we each witness through half glimpses and nearly shut eyes the light in the room fade from the lakefront's vibrant, eminent dark to a clouded half light. I'm still a little drunk. I roll off the bed and try to make little noise as I go to vomit in the toilet. My head hits something on the way to the bathroom. I kneel and vomit black something into the toilet. I cup my hands under the sink and drink water out of them. I go back in bed but it is very uncomfortable. Elle looks like her body is twisted into an impossible position. I sit in bed next to Chloe and wait for the two of them to wake up. They never do. I pace the room and try to sleep on the floor and then I go to the bathroom and puke again. I feel like killing something or something like that. I feel extremely desperate. My hands and the bed and Chloe and Elle are spotted with mud. I put my shorts on and I put my dress on. The room has taken on a quality of brownness and dust. I remember Chloe and Elle's performance art piece two months ago and I feel embarassed for them and repulsed by them. I wait for them to wake up. I try to move the bed in a way that seems unintentional. I find ketamine on the floor and put it in my pocket. I read a book on the nightstand. I pretend I'm somewhere else. Neither of them moves. They stay in bed pretending to be asleep so they won't have to deal with life and the consequences of everything that happened last night, not just the sex.

How much is too much?

from NOTHING IS MISSING

Gr Keer

the attendant tends the exit
to facilitate movement from here to there.
the attendant beckons, disturbs
the atmosphere, provides direction.
the attendant makes change, balances
accounts the attendant disappears
the trail when you're gone.
the attendant declares, a
miscalculation. this,
misapprehends,
what is this that disrupts back
it wants saying.

this is the distance
between points. this
is not a line. this is how even
your body[ ] defies
the significance of architecture

i too am formless

even in forgiveness. i forgive

the body. nothing is

missing.

when you ask for clarity

i ask. we desire the same.

every inch of us

is covered in graffiti.

a marked space can only be tended

until the multiplicity runs

out of desire

so when they say an increase

do they mean an increase in simple mistakes

of the light

smudged where it meets

blood flow

what is blood

flow and what liquid

wants to. you taste

like want to

and graffiti.

so much want to missing

the body shifts of its own volition

when your face opens

color falls out

such a muscular mouthful

a confident production

the body shifts open

when silken efficiency

how we talk to each other

when is this physics is

so much rainbows

nothing wished for

so much want to

so much want to missing

the body shifts back on its open

with troubling efficiency

color of meat and wishes

color of want to

so much physics so much have to

so much silken muscle so much

open

shifting the

nothing

i went pretty far and came back

i went pretty far until

you yourself grow lined

what does it say there

i went pretty

into your darkest places

i went pretty far there and then

a thousand details i never knew

i needed

i missed you to a point

no longer the mountain no longer the ocean

[i am] still [moving] there

we were all there

under the hot black sky   listening

so many shifting bodies like water

we felt words rise like steam

words like stars swimming in a black pool

it's hot there when it's hot

all our molecules were dancing like steam off a black starry pool

shifting bodies dancing into the night under stars

raining down from rooftops like falling

embers from the blackened night sky

hot bodies drenched in the universe falling from the sky

when words hit your skin it melted leaving only your clothes to

mark your passing

that night we were a body unquestioned

all our molecules were ecstatic fire

IF SHE ALWAYS
Grey Vild

If she always

      gets what she wants,
            sooner or later she wants what she gets.

If the mouth in the mirror
        fails to move,
             the salamander smiles,
                too soon.

If the tabby in the woodpile cries,
        the air breaks off
             tiny knucklebones scatter the yard.

If there is an earthquake in East Cleveland,
        we forget
            every time
           we tie our skates
to stone floor so crushing,
        he winds the clock
             every time
           he comes home.

If he tries to swim,
             he will drown.

If the boys bark,
        chase the squirrels away
                      a cardinal's flight pock-marks
                          our blue window.

If she always wants what she gets   no one can be blamed
the river burned—
                        he will drink the water.

If they race to fill the old woman's lap
                with apples,
                        we play catch
                across the evening traffic.

If he disappears in an old nirvana t-shirt,
                      there is always the woods
                  between here and the party
If not the abandoned school bus,
        the little booth above the bleachers,
                        echo the static.

If no one cheers,
                      someone still wins.

If not no,
                                yes.

If not now,
                                now.

If the drive home swallows frozen,
                glass-stubbled fields,
                          please,
                                  be late to pick me up.

If no one is to blame,
                          she wants it every time.

If the cold is thick enough,
                          he will split it like an axe.

If wine garnets the twist of her lips,
                fits leather to her teeth,
                        she will laugh and laugh and laugh

when she catches him
            studying to be beautiful,
                      he will still get away with everything.

If she obsesses over him,
                        it's best if he's already dead.

If he traverses a tar-softened summer
            its hollow where every shell rests,
                          an ocean crashes
                          the bulb of the head.

If a certain substance in the palm
                foams like power,
                              a hinge rusts shut
                              a body.

A DISGUST

A disgust   and a lack
a body   that vacates   a body

that is comprised   primarily   of cleaning products!

I was jealous when he died,
and not of death.

The stainless steel surface wiped clean,
                                    it will have to be wiped again,
                                                            and soon.

                                    Does anyone live in a dream?
                                    Is that alive,
                                            where dreaming is?

                                            a mother's jewelbox
                                                    yr
                                            mother's
                                                    jewelbox
                                                            heheheh

                                        and it was on fire.
                                        or
                                              the forest.
                                        of course.

I have no altar,
            can I borrow yours?

        I have no robe,
                    may I,
                            please?
And that one,
            too.

                                                        Just
                                            Keep 'em moist
                                                    I think
                                        You can handle that.

SOUND THE OCEAN

Slam the bathroom door.

                                                              The shadow
                                          box
                                  falls
                                          all the shells
                                break
                            and
                                      the shadows.

None of them
    sound the ocean
anyway.

                            Carve
              a groove
                            in a groove
      of wood grain
with a broad,
         flat thumb
                never
     broad or flat
enough
             even these,
                          strangely
                  delicate.

STATICS

my window
is lit
the smallest,

the pane
cold,
no frost yet flicks,
flickers

a nerve, statics
a balloon
where I should be

Please,

Don't love me
or anyone else.

Thanks!

She reads
theory for poetry
and
poetry for theory.

          I lie
         to everyone,
         unironically,

           left a note:

  just keep 'em moist

       I think I watered them once
          and forgot.

Is a preserved and natural sense of curiosity the same thing as a
         healthy sex drive?

AN ELEGANT REFUSAL

She's the one
    with the Darger tattoo
            without any penises —
                what's the point of that?

           The dark meat
                reminds her
              of cadavers
       sighs

When no one
    is around

              we are
      a house   of sighing
   no one hears.

   A body
produces   muscles
    that adhere
      even
        when
     a   no
      is   loud
    enough.

    No
public   secret
                      hovers on
            No
      erotics
   of
torture.

            Pay close   attention
                           and a
                              long,
                                  slight
                                neck.

                 An elegant
                            refusal
                   may be
                         all you get.

I don't think
                I was a little boy
                    or
                a little girl.
  I was just terrified.

No   that can't be right.

WITH THE NERVES LIT

A ritual
                        is mostly
                                            absence.

               And we!
               Are free!

Every! Time!
               I walk into
                        the subway,
                     Jack and Jill
                     there,
                              smiling.

                            And I'm
                            the
                                  trick
                   passing
                      at the horizon,
                              nothing happens.

Here, where
                 you were born,
                     Marianne.

A tradition
         when,
                  your face falls
                           when,
                                    your face
                                    is held up
                                             bright

with the nerves,
         lit.

Can terror be
                                             a gender?

Will my father be
                                             forever tired?

I
    will
         be
                  a   man
                  then
                           a
                                    variety
                                    of
                                             compulsions.

I AM NOT TALKING ABOUT GAY MARRIAGE

H. Melt

March 27, 2013

"It was agreed that featuring American flags at our program was the best way to illustrate this unifying issue"

Human Rights Campaign

karin quimby, a blonde haired white woman
working for the human rights campain

told Bryan Ellicott, a bisexual trans man
to stop waving the trans flag

outside the supreme court
after asking what it represents

an unidentified videographer
threatened to burn it

wanted to edit us
out of the frame

only american flags

allowed on capitol

over the hill

I burn

american flags

in my dreams

I burn

white dresses

honeymoon suites

red roses on the bed

bloody sex

on the first night

you die a little

MAYBE A LITTLE GIRL WILL KILL ME TOMORROW

Janani Balasubramanian

tw: *suicide, murder, death*

I started thinking about killing myself
when I was five.
Not about killing myself as I was,
cute and full of possibility,
but about killing an
older, taller version,
maybe one with longer hair,
or none at all.
I would never see myself coming,
loom outside
police cars hovering past,
they would never suspect the palm tree kid,
the balloon pants,
the toy pistol and the real knife.
2030, you see, will be a simpler time,
where murder only happens under state surveillance,

where the hemlock is grown on the white house lawn,

where we have robots to do all the dirty work,

where everything is that much more honest.

Five year old me would sidle up next to the house I'd live in,

look through a window at my lover

give myself imploring eyes

like there's something I need to tell you.

Tonight I need to kill you.

Tonight I need to be a little girl who kills you.

I figured this way

I would know when I will die,

and how,

and who would do it,

that I would die

at the hands of a good kid

at least,

and I would live to just under 40,

like any good short story.

It would be the perfect blend of

murder and suicide,

the consent written long ago.

I wonder sometimes if I've done it,
if time travel comes with
its own kind of amnesia.
Is it like being black-out drunk?
Is it like that?
Will you tell yourself about it later?
Like hey, you were
mad funny in the 1980s.
And the times we had in the precambrian,
oh man.
And if time-travel
is like being black-out drunk,
then I probably didn't
walk in a straight line
and I probably
landed wrong.

I have all these patchy memories
of New York in the 1860s,
all the bustle
and the abolitionists
and poor dusty white kids in gray caps
and the animals!

New York City was a zoo back then;
pigs, dogs, monkeys,
even some cross-bred thing like a
tunafish with hands.
Old police journals will say things like
"oh I spotted some colored women today
and a tunafish with hands".

I have also seen Gandhi
reach the great saltlicker ocean,
and Hildegaard of Bingen
invent marijuana,
and the Mesopotamians
invent a universe from a castrated god,
and lots of unnamed people run
in a revolution
though I'm not sure where.

When you're in kindergarten,
and think the universe
is a conspiracy of microcuts
that life
is a series of meaningless poses

they tell you you're so

imaginative

or gifted.

They give you

a new library card,

and a crayon.

No one can really be that bitter or sad

they think without having lived

for millenia first.

It's easier to believe

that children are born

angelic and empty

rather than hardened

by the violence

enacted against

their many

many mothers.

While you were kicking and screaming

there was a genocide happening

just two centuries prior,

maybe a famine,

and a war across the world at the same time.

We are all here

because our ancestors

did things

to survive,

and because we did things

to survive.

Because our mother's wombs

are where we first learn

to be violent,

because we scratched

and ate them

dry and red.

Because we

swallow history whole

and cannot birth it away.

And maybe a little girl

will kill me tomorrow.

ALLEYWAY
j/j hastain

Because T had never thought of an alleyway as a place to fuck, had never had her own pages burned in front of her face as a form of unfettering violence, there were definite differences between us. The evening when I took her into the alleyway and fucked her with my fingers and an old, tattered, linen copy of Lorca's poems, I saw her eyes buzz at the same time that they were burning; saw the sound of bustling retinas.

Sensing moments by way of a contagious clout (by miasmatic vibrations) can actually stabilize some of the aspects of us which are not yet birthed. The buzz induces marvelous causation: pronounces the shape of tender, motile length. An untamed, peristaltic neck? Precursor to her future, queer genital?

We were burning in a cramped space wherein pressure was being felt as a form of pleasure. Is there an alley behind your house? Alleys are turning into allies as we burn in them like pages passionately caught in an updraft which began on and begets the city street. I am vitalized by supporting the protrusions of growing things with pages upon pages in consecrated dedication to them. This is the what, why and how wherein the primary focus of a previous devotion dies into new form, into organic future.

GETTING TO KNOW YOU

Getting to know the person to whom you are bound, after you are bound and monogamously committed is an interesting twist in the average approaches to monogamy in America. Having been given the image of us (early on) in the form of Vladamir Kush paintings (especially the one where the two lovers are embedded together in the still sealed, hearty nut) I trusted T before I even knew her.

When I say "T" here that is not a stand in for a hidden name. It is what I call her even to this day. T means many things to me. T: (this woman's) testosterone. The secret, sacred unfurl of a lesbian turned queer (by way of interaction with me) woman's testosterone. This woman's testosterone exceeds traditional models of masculinity. T: the birth of the deep life of tea (that oh so human and very green reality) in me.

As someone who was raised Mormon I never had tea when I was growing up. Due to that fact (not having tasted it early on) it did not even cross my mind to drink tea after I left the Mormon Church. Perhaps I was too busy eating and drinking almost nothing to realize that the slow steep of all teas, the theatrical history of puerrh tea (that it must be buried or rot (like compost)), the aroma of lavender flowers wafting from a thick black base of liquid, pulling rose heads out of the steeping pot to let them free in the river, the fact that mixing cinnamon chips and cocoa nibs or fennel and anise would result in such euphoric, embodied elation for me.

"UNDER THE FULL MOONLIGHT WE DANCE"

I was driving with my head in her lap. We were rounding the tight bends of the highway leading between Estes Park National Forest and our home. The light was coming in in little purring spews: it was so full that the moon almost seemed furry. I began to sing easefully: "Under the full moon light we dance, spirits dance we dance, holding hands we dance, joining souls rejoice." I had never heard this song and even though that was the case I joined right in.

As I sang I recalled my resistance to playing double stops when I was learning violin (from child into my teen years). I would mumble little frustrations: "Why do I have to play the melody and the harmony? I want to be playing with someone else, not responsible for holding the whole scale myself." Double stops offended me. I did not come into form to play with myself.

An infinite number of chakras hang on the thick boughs of these bowing trees. The chakras aren't in an upward sloped line anymore: they are scattered, interactive, and they pump as they morph from glistening bowls to glistening female-he phalluses. Round can become elongated can become round. The infinite chakras are composite-consciousness from other lifetimes; they are shape-shifting, hormonal homes: patchwork quills passing through many phases of the moon at once. Will the chakras of *else* run our genders amok? Will we be enabled by that?

Because I was falling more in love with T, I was certainly coming into deepening love of the moon, although I was aware as we passed this harmony through each other, weaving it, that I could not identify with the moon until I knew it as cream and cayenne, both: red organs rolled tightly into white drapes then unrolled with drape and organ lifted.

Dear Beloved: we embody a contact high and we carry it all the way through a scavenging night sky. We do this while embodying aporia: the chosen abyss of indelible spore-lore. We do this even as subliminal genitals come in to take us over.

LETTER TO THE RADFEMS

Joy Ladin

You're right: there is no me.
I have no history,
no family tree of causes and effects, no unequivocal trace,
no epistemic horizon.

Even now, when I am here, hurling polysyllabic abstractions
to prove how smart I am,
I am a matter of dispute, a misunderstanding, a bundle
      of unverifiable claims
about feelings you cannot imagine,

a shorting of binary circuits
glittering like a Foucauldian amusement park at night
reflected in the ahistorical water,
in which I, this ahistorical "I,"

glide like a ray, or bob like garbage scow.
I may not be pretty,
but I have a will, and this is it,
a will that has been characterized, in print

as "a type of amorality" embodied
by "a man with enlarged breasts,"
"a truly minor poet," "autogynephiliac," "misogynist,"
a naïve reproduction of "banal cliches of gender,"

a pronoun-challenged dress-up game
that insists "it"
is.
"It" has a will, and this is it:

May you always see yourselves
as fairest in the land,
the most aggrieved, oppressed, authentic,

may binaries blossom in your follicles and fingertips
until you can't conceive good without evil, life without death,
self without the others you disdain

to share your gender with.

May otherness multiply like Pharaoh's frogs

under your covers, between your ribs.

may you who deny that I am I

feel your own "I" split

until you find my pain in your pain,

my heart in your heart.

GLITTER ON THE DANCE FLOOR
Levi Sable

That feeling.

B hated that feeling.

When bodies, swaying to the beat like pendulums, stop, the last notes of music trailing out into the Black. When the Pteridophyta DJ with the endless eyes and the feather-light finger-leaves darkens his equipment, disappearing into a throng towards the bar. When the bar's owner, or as B calls him, boss, begins switching over the equipment to the Bot DJ. The dance floor more or less cleared, everyone shifting their masses towards the bar, towards a table, towards the antigravity playground. In the middle of that emptiness B stood, hands hitched in their pockets, hating that feeling, that endless, purposeless drifting—go? Stay? As if this decision was one of mind-boggling finality.

They usually went home. Sometimes they drank, but by the time most of the bar's cocktails oozed into their brain they were bored and on their way back to their quarters anyway. Concoctions that sped up the inebriation process cost too much, even with B's discount. But what else was there to do, on this spinning pit-stop for the fabulous and free, for those with papers and those without, equally? Drink, dance, and then leave the next morning, with a story and a hangover.

But not B. B never left. They were staff, and this was their home, their living, their escape and prison, lashed together on a spinning mineral deposit in the middle of the Black. They were done with the vengeful punishment that had launched them from the homeworld out here. They could hitch a ride, sure, but where was there to go?

Anyway, they had to report for work the next morning.

Idly they walked worn flooring to the edge of the dance floor. It was in the center of the great big club. In one corner the bar lurked; Bots flittered overhead, taking orders or delivering drinks, while the new 'Sapien bartender flashed smiles and bottles and a cybernetic third arm. In another corner, the requisite anti-gravity playground, with its flashing lights and strange apparatus, . There were tables and couches for all sorts of body types. Stragglers stood on the dance floor, still, groups with tentacles twined or more mammalian limbs pressed and searching. Watching them, B almost felt lonely, but the feeling passed quickly enough. They just ached to dance some more.

A nervous, penned animal, they finally made a decision and settled at an empty table littered with cups and crushed napkins and a trail of roasted berries. The berries were an experiment. A few weeks ago, their regular dish had been roasted larvae, so crispy and sweet. But then, some Arthropod or another had taken offense at being served their cousin's children, the bartender had been shot, and several of B's Bot servers, too. And now it was a plant-only establishment.

Even the staff had their nutritional needs met through protein packs now. B missed the taste of real food more than ever. Such items could be purchased illegally for exorbitant cost, and the scent of such contraband, sizzling sausages or roasting poultry, would waft its way through the ventilation system, waking B in the middle of the night, trying to eat their thin little pillow.

Voices and creatures blurred by, and B let the noise flow over them, enjoying the solitude at the table of trash. On the other side of the dance floor, there was a blue spark, a series of incomprehensible swearwords from their boss, and the lights dimmed for a second. B chuckled, and unfocused again.

Focus came on the swishing of four legs, as Doza, the 'Phyta DJ, came to rest on the settee next to them. He clacked his face-fronds together loudly, the sound like sticks knocking against each other, a friendly greeting for a 'Phyta. B and Doza had never been face to face, though Doza had been their guest DJ for a few weeks already—their lives were in very different parts of the club.

Doza had a docked ship; B, a small room far beneath all of that. Doza was up all night, and as a 'Phyta, slept under a sunlight all day. But beyond that basic understanding of biology, B knew next to nothing about Pteridophyta. Doza's face was strangely grayish green, and shimmery. His mouth peeked out from beneath a bush of thin, white, root-like tendrils. The two big fronds, studded with little feathery leaves, flanked either side of that mouth.

B nodded courteously. "Thanks for the set. You're great."

Doza clacked again. Not having the equipment to vocalize, he didn't—but 'Phyta were mildly telepathic, and Doza's response appeared quite efficiently in B's mind. *Aim to please. You work here, yes?*

B nodded again. "Robot maintenance. How much longer are you staying?"

Leave tomorrow.

"That's too bad. I was really enjoying your music. Well, thank you for brightening up this rock."

Doza clattered excitedly. *Looking forward to moving. Not for staying in one place. Might put down roots.* And then his fronds began vibrating, and B realized he was laughing.

B laughed too. "That might be dangerous."

Very happy you're happy, though. His dark eyes flitted around the room. *Thought I had companion for tonight. Feeling I might be stood up.*

B looked around, mildly surprised. "I hadn't seen another 'Phyta tonight." Most of their clientele were solidly mammalian—'Sapiens, usually.

Doza's fronds waved gently. *Not 'Phyta. 'Sapiens.*

B squinted at him. "Sorry for assuming. I hadn't realized that was possible."

Doza's eyes still scanned the waiting crowd. *When 'Phyta-'Phyta mate, those-with-tendrils-without-pods inject willing those-with-pods-without-tendrils with special tendril. Is full of drug. Injection makes everyone happy. Works same way, without pods, when 'Phyta-with-tendrils-without-pods mate with anyone else. 'Pods. 'Sapiens. Chemical works on just about everyone. Phyta-and-mate think together. Real pretty. Real good.*

B let this all sink in. Doza's thoughts had been a little hard to follow, the vocabulary obviously foreign—but they got the idea. "I agree. Sounds real good."

Doza clacked gently again, his eyes focusing on B's own. Their two dark eyes, big nose, and brown skin reflected strangely blurred in Doza's dark eyes. *Nice girl wanted a try, said I would meet after. I think she's gone.*

B stood up. "I'm thirsty. You need anything?"

No, but kindness is appreciated.

"Don't go too far."

Doza clacked acknowledgment.

B got a bubbly liquid called "Hyd-Now!" Their boss had bought it from some traveling merchant who guaranteed it was worth its weight in chips on the richer worlds. Six months later, and it was always on sale, in order that they could get it out of their stores. They could barely give the stuff away.

It came in a short, fat, cylindrical cup. They took a mouthful and turned back to their companion. Doza looked on over the dance floor, four legs and two arms relaxed, dotted with tough, fern-like fingers. His body was long and bulbous and glittered and gleamed faintly in the club's dim light. His body was grayish, dark and massive.

B took another mouthful of Hyd-Now!, the moisture flooding their mouth and settling the tiny, nervous knot in their stomach. It was fizzy, a little like tart fruit and a little like honey, with a complex, musky aftertaste. A little like overripe fruit. After buying it they always remembered that bit.

As they approached the table, the 'Bot was (finally!) hooked up. Music flooded in, the Bot shouted a bedazzling introduction (the same introduction it shouted every night) and began to throw out some canned tunes (the same tunes it produced every night). B wanted to care what had gone wrong—but they didn't. B and Doza watched the mass of people flood onto the floor, the unblinking, rainbow eyes of the Bot DJ hovering above them.

B almost followed.

Instead, they sat back down next to Doza, and together they watched the crowd, as B sipped.

"How long does it last?"

A few hours.

B shifted, finished his drink.

"I'm interested, if you'll have me."

In the moment that followed, B realized that Doza had never actually asked them, and a fear of rejection rose up in them that was so knee-knockingly physical that B almost ran away, just then. They regretted both the fluid churning now inside their stomach, and that it hadn't been something much, much stronger.

I do not know what gender to refer to you as. The words in B's mind were hesitant and beautiful and welcome.

"I consider myself androgyne. I avoid gendered terms."

Doza clacked. *I understand. You—you make more sense, now.*

B looked down at their body—soft, neither curvy nor flat, comfortably chubby. Mostly hairless, but hairier than many 'Sapiens. Capable hands, but not big ones. Comfortable clothes that did not cling, but were not too big, either, covering up any telltale sex characteristics. Yes. They made sense.

Doza touched them with one soft leafy finger, a trailing touch over their wrist. Doza's touch was almost sticky, like tightly woven, furred fiber. *I have a room reserved, would you feel comfortable...*

B smiled a little shakily, stood up, and stepped aside. "Lead the way!"

They followed the shadows, past the main dance area, dark and dim ghosts among more luminous sprites, out of sync in the throb of bodies. They could feel the atmosphere shift as they neared the antigravity playground, where a few remaining floaters held hands and giggled from the ceiling, and one of the little safety Bots whirred nervously nearby.

Beyond that, rows of rentable rooms stretched down a long hallway. By the hour, by the day. Doza passed an arm over one of the doors. It hissed open, and Doza and B stepped into the darkness. After the door hissed shut, Doza turned on the light, and B was momentarily blinded. When their eyes adjusted, the first thing they saw was Doza's tail.

B had never seen him well-illuminated. They had never noticed the tail, not once (and though it held no special significance, how had they completely missed...?). It was thick and studded with bumps, tap-root-like. His skin was much more leathery and green in the light, and it sparkled like cosmic dust. His eyes were still fathomless, and they were looking B up and down, too, examining them. They supposed they passed muster, because he thudded his tail against the ground as he clacked his fronds, and walked up to the bed.

Glancing slowly around the room, B could tell this one had been designed for 'Phyta. The Bots cleaned these, of course, but B never actually went into them. A half dozen small fountains dotted the walls, trickling quietly to themselves. The room was long and narrow, made longer by the mirrors surrounding the platformed bed at one end. A set of low steps lead up to a bed, glossy blankets and pillow piled high in metallic-shimmery reds and greens.

B sat down on a small chair, colored green and made of some translucent polymer. With shaking hands, they took off their boots. The walls, ceiling, and floor were glaring white, the lights bright, and the temperature close enough to 30°c that B would've been sweating even without feeling nervous.

Can leave clothes on. Whatever is comfortable with you.

B leaned back, socks still on. "I will be more comfortable this way." They removed the long sleeve shirt they were wearing, exposing an undershirt.

Would be most polite, I believe, to explain the entire process before you join me.

B shifted uncomfortably on the sloping chair. "Okay."

Several different chemicals—in stages—involved. First, is a drug that leaches from the fingers, the end of my fronds too. It makes us both relaxed, happy, calm, and comfortable. Usually we use this time to become more well acquainted, to make sure we're both agreeable. As long as we are—we both have the choice to stop—tendril that will unfurl, which will connect us when we want it to. Will pierce your skin. Will be a small cut there, the next morning. After that, we will be unable to stop, until it is done. No harm will come to us. We will share an experience in our minds, together. When out of chemical, my tendril will withdraw itself, and we will likely lose consciousness for a short time. Is that all clear?

"Yes."

Are you okay with proceeding with first stage?

"Yes."

Doza was reclining on his underside, legs stretched out behind him. B stepped up the little steps to the bed, and tried to sit. The sheets were so glossy, and against socks they had little fraction. They half fell, half sat. The bed was soft. The hard shell of the 'Phyta was less so.

"Sorry." B scooted across the bed a little, not yet (ever?) ready to be quiet that on top of him.

Doza waved clacked his fronds in a fast sort of chuckle. The fronds, B noticed up close, were much greener than they'd looked in the club, almost furry as well. Delicately beautiful.

With one long arm, Doza reached out and took B's hand. His temperature was surprisingly warm. Long ago, B had been friends with a Reptilia, a cold blooded friend who had always been chilly, always curling up in the warmest places, against the warmest people. But Doza made his own heat, emanating from him like from a humid jungle. And his thin, furry fingers were soft, and he smelled good.

The music throbbed dully from the dance floor, through the walls and up through their bed, like the most erratic and glorious of heartbeats.

Eyes trained on their face, Doza worked his fronds up B's arm, to the burnt orange cuff of their undershirt, in a strange, gentle massage. Hands still trembling, B reached out to touch the smooth, hard surface of Doza' back, then up, to the back of his head, to his face. His thin, bright green bits had produced tiny droplets. They came off oily on B's fingertips, the scent complicated and flowery, and completely foreign. The droplets of moisture were also springing from Doza's fingertips on B's arm. They wanted to bury themselves in that smell, to coat their room in it, such an organic thing to be there in the Black.

"Much nicer than the fluids 'Sapiens produce," B murmured, eyes half open as they paid attention to their fingers on the 'Phyta's body, the 'Phyta's touch on themself.

Often confused how you evolved to produce such strangely scented sweat.

"I think our noses are not very sensitive."

Doza clattered his fronds. *They are not.*

Focusing on Doza's mouth, B reached out and brushed their fingers over the fine white roots there. They clung to their fingers, tickled, dripped. B laughed delightedly.

Doza's leaves were in B's short hair, pushing it around. *'Sapien hair is always so nice. Simple. Feels good.*

Their arms eventually met, B's fingers working down Doza's leathery skin to the strange fingers, and then, 'Sapien finger explored 'Phyta finger in the most simple and intimate of moments. They both stilled, relishing the lull.

B gave a little sigh, then, and Doza rubbed the soft green things together, the gentlest of noises. *Do you want to continue?*

Should I pierce you now? Doza's words in his mind came slow and calm and a little sleepy.

Not afraid anymore, skin buzzing with the attention and mind stilled, B asked, "Will it hurt?"

A little.

"Where?"

A shoulder will do nicely.

B brought a lazy hand up to their shoulder, pulled aside their collar. "I'm still in."

Already their bodies were intertwined. Doza shifted slightly, so that one of his arms was around B's waist, the other resting on their thigh. He shifted slightly, bearing B's weight, supporting them. The mandible-like fronds on Doza's face parted, and a spindly, delicate tendril unfurled from his face. It brushed their skin, just barely long enough. It was bright, bright green against B's darker, matte skin.

Ready?

"As ever," B said, their heart racing a little as they said it.

The tendril wiggled a bit, reared up a little—B could see it out of the corner of their eye—and then plunged into their skin.

They gasped, the sting flooding their body. It burned, definitely hurting—and then strangely, though it still burned, it did not hurt. And then, though it burned, it was a lovely burn, a rapturous burn.

There was a breath then, or maybe a handful of them, when B felt very little, just a gentle warmth, a numbness, a calm. They were aware of the overwhelming scent and moisture coming from Doza, leaking beautifully out of him. Warmth, the dainty, clear, dirt-like humidity of him.

And then a shudder went through them both and they were back on the dance floor

 and everything glittered like stars

 and the floor burned bright

 and the Black settled in like a 'Phyta's hug, moist and warm and close

 and Doza, inches and miles away, nimbly played tunes through spider's silk, flickering with color. His eyes glittered hard like gems, endless like an ocean, trained on B so that he could see into their soul.

 and B danced, exploding in movement and joy and the beat, the beat, in every inch of their body, seeping through their pores. Their eyes, unable to break away from Doza's, not wanting to, wanting to drink his eyes up through their stare, drink his beat through their skin, like a heartbeat, pounded out by stars.

 there was no one else, of course, no one

but Doza and B and B and Doza, but B danced as if in the middle of a throng of bodies, collective masses bring them into euphoria, an ecstatic purity, and Doza played as if for hundreds, the moment complete, musician and dancer, perfect and forever.

dancing.

dancing.

closer

until B couldn't tell which bit was B and which bit was Doza

until B couldn't tell who was breathing

moving

dancing

in their own skin

Until

Like a deep breath

Like a release

Like an End, a Beginning, a Heartbeat

Doza's thin tendril slipped out of their skin

And B's consciousness slipped out of their body.

And they woke up in their own bed with the alarm going off, their boots neatly set next to the door. They were fully clothed, wrinkled and smelling, delicately, sweetly, of 'Phyta. They pulled them off regretfully and then shoved them under the bed for later. They showered, and before they left, checked the message blinking silently at their terminal.

Thank you. If ever we meet again, I hope we can dance.

With a smile, B went off to work, wondering for how long their room would be infused with Doza's fragrance.

THINGS I WISH I COULD ENJOY AGAIN (BUT HAVE BEEN TAINTED BY AUTISM SPEAKS PROPAGANDA)

Lucas Scheelk

Things I wish I could enjoy again (but have been tainted by Autism Speaks propaganda):

My Sunday in the Park on the Island of La Grande Jatte puzzle. Connecting the dots on a physical level. Visualizing the painting outside of Chicago, and Google. It's collecting dust on the top shelf of my closet.

The color blue. Any shade of blue. I dreamed of having sky blue walls as a child but couldn't because I lived in apartments.

The month of April. That's when the showers begin. The rain is supposed to be enough.

Being myself.

AMERICAN CROW
Mx Glass

a kid in a garbage dump naked film skin except for meager tufts of gray down cry with large thick necked straight bill wingtip feathers spread like fingers ah ah start a hoarse screech as if in pain oh oh from stubbing a toe and capture exhausted birds, catch fish, eat from dog bowls, soon the scavenger sleeps in a commune and lazily steps off the train tracks not worried since he's been reincarnated more times than Shiva, and glares from the corner of his eye at me as he tilts his head ah ha ha he steals food from the gull as the car swerves to hit and misses his ma who kicked him out young with feathers that were still shiny trash bags

ERRARE

I'm trying to create a sentence that doesn't use metaphors. Someone, please, give me a language that's exact. I don't want to believe that life is a fire and a river; that love is a journey and a physical force and a Shakespearean illness. *Errare*: romance's root is to wander and to be wrong. That root is from a rose that is a rose that is a rose that is annoying to perceive–yet its dried yellow petals still burn in my hands when I've scooped them up from around the vase. This photograph on the fridge is you because it is of your face. It wouldn't be you if it was a snapshot of your mouth, and it isn't you now. I want to say "I'm in love with you." But, I am floundering in this, in this, in this, because metaphors are the deep end, are Hallmark cards, are crowded train cars, are trap doors.

ARCHITECTURE
reba overkill

this one is for my folk who were built to hate ourselves.
we had no hammers in our hands but everything that we heard,
each eye we caught and mouth we turned downward, we learned.
the stone and glass rose up around us and we found out that you
keep breathing even when there is no light and plaster won't stop
handling you greedily. how did these walls grow around us? but,
i see us trying. i see us kicking holes in hollow halls and using
everything we can break as footholds. but it's okay, please know,
if you are stuck, if you feel casket-bound. i don't have to be brave.
but maybe today i will be brave. you don't have to be brave.
keep an eye out for cracks in your cage and if you can,
press your ear to the wall. i've got handsaws, i've got fingernails,
and i'm looking for you. someone wants to make you safe.
just keep breathing. someone's coming.

ROUND, HOPEFUL POEM

i can't tell you how i know
just hold my swollen
assurances like
fat little toads
small things
meant well
i promised
curvatures
let me say
my body is
given haven
i'll match your
cold, lonely parts
with my honest skin
i can warm and remind you

MY POWERS ARE AWAKENING

now accepting applications for worshipers
i've won fifteen straight games of freecell
but all i want is some devout disciples
build a shrine to me, i'll send you hair
and i'll tell you everything you didn't know
you needed me to tell you. start with a
postcard. write in your favorite ink.
send your poem of a prayer, tell me
you need your god/dess. tell me why.
i promise not to send you to hell
esoteric emotional exchanges e-wait u

ART AND SEX ALONG THE NEW YORK WATERFRONT

Rex Leonowicz

after a multimedia art exhibit at the leslie lohman museum for gay and lesbian art

no white gay men
naked by the thousands
on the piers anymore, but
there are exhibits
we can count on,
the photos mounted
on canal st.

what does it mean
for a community pushed
out of itself
to not see itself.
all the femme queen
bodies have drifted
out to sea, not bumping

up on the docks anymore.
the hudson's current
swift change
drowning out difference.

these are the same
streets, the same
symbols—the plaster
keeps the same
white cast, flags
of six colors flap
in the white sky.

the one brown body:
an oiled torso, faceless
photo named "dark boy bathing."
stark-bodied boy wonders,
posthumous art stars,
scroll the walls:
in memory of   in memory of

where are your feelings?
locate them.
do not analyze. locate.

are they in your heart, your stomach, your lungs?

do not analyze... locate.

i imagine a gummy plush squish of my lungs, the synthetic binding compression squeezing past industrial muscle to bruise bubblegum pink to a rotting purple. my lungs: where i feel everything collapsing in on itself. my breasts made flat by threads sewn together, how is that even possible? flat in a way that no one could anticipate what they might look like. surprise. flat in a way that knocks out breath.

but, relocate: the feelings of my chest. bruises would form first on the ribs, not the lungs. remember ribs as more than compact bone, but also the meat of tissue around bone and intercostal nerves, nerves that web-between. first the ribs bruise and maybe swell, and then the ribs might transition, change shape, move. compress til misshapen, til closing in on the lung, so the bone becomes the textile pressing into lung as synthetic mesh presses into the breasts.

do not analyze: think smaller. to the surface of skin and just under it. too much pressure for too long a duration, can impair receptive nerves in the nipple; maybe loss of sensation. wasn't the point of keeping them: sensation? i haven't felt erogenous in eleven months. i've felt erogenous every day for eleven months. wait, do not analyze.

locate: under skin, thin blood vessels pressurized. the supple sponge of breast tissue compressed. blood flow slows first, then clots of cells build up in thin vessels getting thinner, weaving themselves to the heart.

relocate: the heart. human, crucial fist of muscle, pump of meat clenching and unclenching, performing its nature to circulate, keep un-stagnant. the heart banging blood on the cave walls of my ears when my face burns, cheeks ruddied by dried streambeds of tears. searing hurt to the confined heart. i can't love you. i feel it here.

This Year When Sharon Olds Won the Pulitzer No One Seemed to Remember or Care That She Once Published a Poem about Trans Women's "Chopped Off" Penises That Participated in a Transphobic Feminist Politics Which Argues That All Trans People But Especially Trans Women Should Be Morally Mandated Out of Existence

Stephen Ira

Naturally, their virtuosity is beyond your luck—with medicine

at least. They are not cut but tucked up inside—see,

I won't even let you be evil, just naïve.

This poem is tossed off because so was yours,

lazily unsutured like you, incomplete without its ending,

where the penises rise up to live in peace

on the bodies of scandalized cis women walking by.

I used to dream about this as a boy;

when it was done, I'd watch like "you got what you wanted"—

now you have a whole gender to break out of, all your own.

FOUR YEARS
Van Binfa

my mother went from calling me a freak
to sticking a syringe full of testosterone
into the fleshy part of my ass

in just four years

she watched me
try and stick myself
in my thighs
two weeks ago
and i couldn't
it hurt too much

she mutters that she can't understand
why they can't make smaller needles
she says it hurts her to cause me pain

and i want to tell her

momma

mami

mama

i've been in pain for a long time

i appreciate choosing which pain to be in

thigh or ass

i'll take ass

remember when i was thirteen

and you wouldn't let me shave my legs

because you thought that was growing up too fast

but i was so hairy momma and the blond skinny white girls

were so not and i wanted so badly to be like them

i felt pain then

remember when i was eighteen

and i got my first job and worked with these girls

three, four years older and they wore makeup like

it would expire soon

and the uniform looked cute on them

because they had curves

and i got called sir all the time

i tried so hard

put big earrings on

padded my bra

smiled more

and i felt like such a failure still

because i had broad shoulders

hair everywhere

no breasts

no ass

how was i supposed to be a girl

when i hardly felt or looked like one

i felt pain then

remember when you called me a freak

told me to get out

i wasn't natural

que nadie aqui va ser asi

remember two days ago

when this big white man at a gas station

looked at me like he wanted to hurt and laugh at me

simultaneously

remember here
and here
and there

scars from my own hands
pin pricks from previous shots
bruises from who knows what

remember me
trying to explain to a date
exactly who and what i am
and they lose all interest
too much of a boy
not enough of a girl
too much of a girl
not enough of a boy

remember that mom
the looks
the stares
the questions

remember nurses in the hospital

when i had cancer

asking me if i was there for a sex change

remember being ignored the first few times

i pushed the call button on the ob/gyn floor

after my hysterectomy

remember the first time, mom

that you stood up for me

in the ER

all 5'4" of you

at two in the morning when the doctor on call

wouldn't stop hurting me with a pap smear

wouldn't stop when i said no more

wouldn't stop when i cried out

you said get out

stop touching my son

i'm taking him home

remember the first time your daughter died

because you let her go

your son needed you

pink hair and painted nails and all

needed you

still does

remember when i was twenty-five and you

brought home your friend and introduced me

as your son, your best friend, your man of la casa

and i said, ma don't embarrass me!

momma

mami

mama

my life has been about a lot of pain

but with you here

and that needle in my ass

dios mio mami

sometimes

i never thought i would make it

sometimes

i still don't

pero aqui tu estas

viejita linda

despues de todo eso

after all that

who knew, mom

that pain would make me so filled with wonder.

CONTRIBUTORS

Boston Davis Bostian is a poet, writer, speaker, facilitator, and future librarian. His current project is a trilogy of poetry manuscripts titled TransPoetica: Journal of Ashes. The first of the series, The Pre-Op Version, removes the masks of grieving the pre-transition self and the rejected and questioning self. The Post-Op Version and The Final Cut, volumes two and three of the TransPoetica Series, will seek to embrace surrender of the evidential self. Boston received a creative writing degree in poetry from the University of Houston Main Campus. He was a founding co-creator of The GENDER Book Project where he held the position of Co-Creator and Project Writer. Additional projects include: Define TraNsition, a portrait-based collection of definition, reconstruction, and transformation informed by Boston's poem "Define TraNsition" and in collaboration with photographer Jan Johnson. Define TraNsition serves as a work sample prelude to his partnership with photographer Jan Johnson; their forthcoming project is Southern TraNsition, a book format collection of poetry and photography that serves to traverse, document, and question inherited and restrictive view resulting from traditional southern representation of gender archetypes as it relates to transgender, gender diverse, and gender independent individuals. Boston is the current lead facilitator of Genderpedia.net and a co-facilitator of the upcoming reading series: Indie Penned Events' Poetry to Portrait Series at Independence Art Studios in Houston, TX. His work can be found at www.bostondavisbostian.com.

Brody Wood is a writer, performer and teacher living in Maine. They care about radical support networks and healing from chronic pain. They are enchanted by country, math, crying, and football. They can be found at brodyxwood.com.

Calvin Gimpelevich is queer and queer and queer. His work appears in Gravel, The Collection, Best Gay Erotica, and Best Lesbian Erotica. He writes for Wolfmen, a trans-themed comic online. Find him at wolfmencomic.com.

Cassady Bee is a queer/genderqueer person finding meaning in their connections with others and the support they can bring to the various communities they are a part of. Using they/their/them pronouns makes them happy, as does writing a poem that lasts.

Codi Suzanne Oliver has written stories and has contributed to blogs, all of which can be found at codisuzanneoliver.blogspot.com

Willow Healey is just another part-time writer who spends a lot of time hanging out with bugs. She blogs things at witchybullshit.tumblr.com

Gr Keer is a trans poet librarian living in Oakland, CA. Their work has appeared in Troubling the Line: Trans and Genderqueer Poetry and Poetics and poeticdiversity: the litzine of los angeles, as well as in their 2013 chapbook, Heterotextual.

Grey Vild's work has been best described as sitting in the closet, dittling itself, and, like, you know, frying baloney on a light bulb.

H. Melt is a poet and artist who was born in Chicago. Their work proudly documents Chicago's queer and trans communities. They are a writer for Original Plumbing, teaching artist, and author of SIRvival in the Second City: Transqueer Chicago Poems.

Janani Balasubramanian is a South Asian literary and performance artist based in Brooklyn. Their work deals broadly with themes of empire, desire, ancestry, microflora, apocalypse, and the Future. Janani is one-half of the spoken word duo DarkMatter and a designer at the RootSpace Collective. They also write for Black Girl Dangerous, an online forum for queer and trans* people of color. You can read more of Janani's work at queerdarkenergy.com.

j/j hastain is a queer, mystic, seer, singer, photographer, lover, priest/ess, and writer. As artist and activist of the audible, j/j is the author of several cross-genre books and enjoys ceremonial performances in an ongoing project regarding gender, shamanism, eros and embodiments. j/j hastain is the author of several cross-genre books including the trans-genre book libertine monk (Scrambler Press), anti-memoir a vigorous (Black Coffee Press/ Eight Ball Press) and The Xyr Trilogy: a Metaphysical Romance. j/j's writing has most recently appeared in Caketrain, Trickhouse, The Collagist, Housefire, Bombay Gin, Aufgabe and Tarpaulin Sky. j/j has been a guest lecturer at Naropa University, University of Colorado and University of Denver.

Joy Ladin is the author of six books of poetry: last year's The Definition of Joy, Lambda Literary Award finalist Transmigration, Forward Fives award winner Coming to Life, Alternatives to History and The Book of Anna, (all from Sheep Meadow Press), and Psalms (Wipf & Stock). Her memoir of gender transition, Through the Door of Life: A Jewish Journey Between Genders, was a 2012 National Jewish Book Award finalist. Joy's work has appeared and is forthcoming in many periodicals, including American Poetry Review, Prairie Schooner, Southern Review, Parnassus: Poetry in Review, Southwest Review, Michigan Quarterly Review, and North American Review, and has been recognized with a Fulbright Scholarship that enabled her to serve as Poet-in-Residence at Tel Aviv University. Joy holds the David and Ruth Gottesman Chair in English at Stern College of Yeshiva University, and has also taught in the Graduate Program in Creative Writing at Sarah Lawrence College, Princeton University, Tel Aviv University (as Fulbright Poet-in-Residence), Reed College and the University of Massachusetts at Amherst.

Levi Sable is a speculative fiction author, parenting blogger, and devout queer. He lives in Madison, Wisconsin with his partner, child, sister, three cats, and giant dog.

Lucas Scheelk is a white trans* Autistic queer poet from Minneapolis, Minnesota. Lucas uses 'he, him, his' pronouns and 'they, them, their' pronouns.

Mx. Glass has recently graduated from the BA program at San Francisco State University. Xyr current project is to look at different modes of haunting in our society, such as metaphor, gender, trauma, and memory.

hi my name is a reba and i'm a writer because i say so :(rebaoverkill.com

rex leonowicz is a trans intersectional feminist poet from queens, new york. his work explores the politics of public and private space, specifically in relation to how marginal identities and bodies navigate those spaces in the face of rapid gentrification, re-development, and cultural co-optation. he is pursuing his mfa in poetry at mills college, and his work has been featured in lambda literary's poetry spotlight, getrude journal, dude magazine, subtext queer arts magazine, testimony: an exhibit and online gallery of lgbtq arts, among others.

Stephen Ira lives in Yonkers, New York, and has had his poetry, fiction, and political polemic published in Specter Magazine, The Collection: Short Fiction From the Transgender Vanguard, LGBTQ Nation, the St Sebastian Review, and other outlets.

Van Binfa is a queer, Chilean trans* activist, who has worked within and for the Chicago Latin@ community. Van and Ivonne Canellada founded Soy Quien Soy, a trans* empowerment collective based in Pilsen. Van is a board member for The Civil Rights Agenda and The Chicago House. He is passionate about the representation of trans* people of color within queer organizations. Van is also an artist and a writer, whose pieces emphasize positive affirmations and the resilience of trans* people of color. Van believes in the individual, everyday acts of activism.